30 Ways to be debt free

Brand Names

Buy a non-brand name with the same ingredients.

Tip: Look at the label. Often times you are paying for the fancy artwork on the outside of the box.

Bus

Take the bus more often. Think about it: Sure it may take a little bit longer but consider a night you might go out on the town with your friends for a drink.

Why wait for a cab to pick you up when you can use those extra minutes to take a bus downtown? You will also save yourself a few more bucks which can buy you that extra beer and reduce pollution at the same time! There's something to cheers about!

Coffee

Make your coffee at home instead of going out.

Add it up: A mocha at your favorite coffee shop is about $3.50 with tax. That's about $80 a month on coffee! Buy a 1# bag for $12 at the grocery store and some chocolate syrup. You'll be amazed how much cheaper your coffee is!

Staying In

Rent DVDs and stay in for a weekend night with a nice bottle of cheap wine.

Fact:

You can rent a movie and purchase a bottle of inexpensive, great wine for half the price you and your date spend at the movie theatre on tickets alone. And you get the best seat in the house!

Coupons

Use coupons at the grocery store.

Tip: Find out when your grocery store is having double or triple coupon days and maximize the value of your coupon. You can often get your toiletries for next to nothing with this smart tactic that smart housewives have been using for decades.

House Tax

Do a "house tax". Charge everyone at home 50 cents a day. Put it in a jar for a rainy day.

Idea: Notice the things you are saving money on and put that money in a jar. Not only will your savings become a visual reality to you but you can set it aside for a special event, and make getting coffee more of a treat rather than a regular spending habit.

Raises

Save your raises instead of spending them. Put them into your savings account along with your other savings.

Idea:

You have already gotten used to living just fine off the amount you make. Now save so you can pay off that car you are still paying on or save up for that vacation.

Sales

Pay attention to sales at your local supermarket.

Tip:

Especially around the holidays, you may find some great deals. Buy ahead and freeze for busy seasons that you know be harder on the wallet, such as Christmas.

Bulk

Buy in bulk.

Tip:

Items such as toilet paper, paper towels, soaps, detergent, and toiletries...things you will always use...save waste by buying in bulk and save yourself money and the extra trips.

Priorities

Pay yourself last.

Suggestion:

If you are in debt and need to save money, eat, take care of your health, and then pay your bills before buying that concert ticket or going on a party weekend.

Raises

Save your raises instead of spending them. Put them into your savings account along with your other savings.

Idea:

You have already gotten used to living just fine off the amount you make. Now save so you can pay off that car you are still paying on or save up for that vacation.

Carwash

Wash your car yourself instead of going to a carwash.

Tip:

You can save up to $50 for doing it yourself. Make it fun! Play music, get the family or your friends involved.

Concessions

Eat big before going to a sporting event or movie where the cost of concessions is the bulk of the price.

Fact: Often the places holding the event, like the movie theatre, have to pay for the movie to be shown or the event to happen at their venue and still can't cover the cost of the tickets.

Concessions are so expensive because of the venues need to make up the difference and actually make a profit.

Leaving

Turn off your AC or heat when leaving the house.

Tip: Put a reminder on your door. For every one degree you save 3% of your energy.

That's a lot!

Eating Out

Share meals!

Tip:

Places like Chinese, Thai, or Italian restaurants are great examples of places to share meals. You usually end up taking home half the food anyway! And if you're still hungry, you can always order more.

Yard Work

Do your own lawn maintenance and mowing.

Tip: Save $50-$100 on hiring someone else and enjoy the sunshine and workout or hire the neighbor boy and give him $20.

Credit Cards

Negotiate your credit card APR rate.

Tip: Too often we settle into rates and allow time to go by. Try calling your card company and find out if there is a way to switch to a lower APR and you may be surprised.

Bad Habits

Reduce the frequency of bad habits...such as eating unhealthy foods, smoking, and drinking alcohol (which are quite spendy).

Tip: Try to do one less cigarette each day or one less beer. You'll be surprised how much you save and how much healthier you will be! Often alcoholic beverages cost more than the meal itself.

Lunch

Make a bag lunch for work.

Suggestion:

Get yourself an insulated container, spoil yourself. Include things you love or make your favorite sandwich, a cup of soup, a little dessert. Make your coworkers jealous they are spending so much and eating so poorly.

Conserve

Tip: Save your plastic sandwich bags and reuse them. Use tupperware instead of a brown bag for work each day.

Use your old shopping bags for waste liners. It not only helps the environment in the end but saves you re-purchasing perfectly reusable items.

TV

Limit your media...Do you really need 300 channels?

Tip:

Very interested in cooking but not in all those extra entertainment programs? Get a smaller package or better yet, get a year subscription to a couple great cooking magazines. Limit your time to watching only an hour a day.

Rewards

Get a credit card that offers rewards.

Tip:

Get rewards that are realistic to your life. Airline flights, deals at the grocery store or places you shop the most.

Interest

Pay off your credit card and stop paying all that interest.

Idea:

Bite the bullet. Get some friends together and think of ways you can save money on the weekends for a month. Try rallying at each of your houses instead of going out. Put the extra money each week towards that huge credit card payment.

Cash

Try to use cash and not credit.

Tip:

This will make what you are spending more of a reality.

Rugs

Add area rugs to hardwood floors to create more warmth and be able to lower your thermostat.

Idea: Area rugs insulate the heat a bit more and also don't make your feet so cold which allows you to keep the chill off a bit more.

Shades

Get reflective window shades.

Fact: Reflective window shades insulates the heat in the winter and reduces the AC costs in the summertime.

Laundry

Wash full loads of laundry instead of half loads and don't use so much detergent.

Idea: Do all your whites one day of the week as well as your colors instead of many little loads. Also reduce the amount of detergent you use. Too much detergent has an opposing effect and also can cause buildup in your washing machine causing it to break down more often.

Shop Therapy

If you must shop for therapy...try somewhere you can get a whole lot more for your buck!

And try not to spend more than $40. Make it a challenge.

Savings

Have savings goals and automatically take that amount out of your paycheck each term for your savings.

Tip: Even if a great concert comes up or an amazing deal on shoes, sacrifice something else to pay for that. Stick to your savings no matter what.

Clutter

Sell that extra clutter you never use on eBay.

Idea: Packrat? There are many all over the world just like you who want to buy your junk that you never use.